S0-AVO-535

A TRUE BOOK™

Women's History in the U.S.

WOMEN in the Civil Rights Movement

Kesha Grant

Children's Press®
An Imprint of Scholastic Inc.

Content Consultant
Holly Hynson, MA
Department of History
University of Maryland, College Park

Thank you to Elise McMullen-Ciotti for her insights into Indigenous Peoples' history and culture.

A CIP catalog record of this book is available from the Library of Congress.
ISBN 978-0-531-13082-7 (library binding) 978-0-531-13341-5 (paperback)

Scholastic Inc., 557 Broadway, New York, NY 10012

1 2 3 4 5 6 7 8 9 10 R 30 29 28 27 26 25 24 23 22 21

Book produced by 22 MEDIAWORKS, INC.
Book design by Amelia Leon / Fabia Wargin Design

Front cover: (clockwise from top left) Daisy Bates, Constance Motley, Jo Ann Robinson, Rosa Parks
Back cover: An African American woman is arrested and carried to a police wagon during a civil rights demonstration in New York in 1963.

Find the Truth

Everything you are about to read is true *except* for one of the sentences on this page.

Which one is **TRUE**?

T or **F** The Montgomery bus boycott was organized by a woman.

T or **F** Daisy Bates was one of three female speakers at the March on Washington for Jobs and Freedom in 1963.

Find the answers in this book.

3

Contents

Protesters from SNCC

The BIG Truth

The March on Washington

Coretta Scott King

No Longer Invisible

The U.S. Constitution guarantees civil rights to all citizens of the United States. Those rights include access to voting and fair and equal treatment under the law. But for nearly a century after the Civil War (1861–1865), African Americans were denied these basic rights. Segregation laws, rules, and customs kept Black people and white people separated throughout the country, especially in the South.

Outraged by these unjust laws, Black leaders organized ordinary people to speak out to achieve equality. **African Americans throughout the country** wrote petitions, protested, and tried to use the law to fight injustice. Black leaders trained activists in important strategies like civil disobedience and nonviolent protest. Organizations like the National Association for the Advancement of Colored People (NAACP) were formed to coordinate protests.

7

All these efforts paved the way for the civil rights movement—a coordinated, mass campaign for equal rights led by African Americans in the **1950s and 1960s.**

Several of the movement's key organizations were founded and led by women. The direction and momentum of the fight for equality would not have been possible without them.

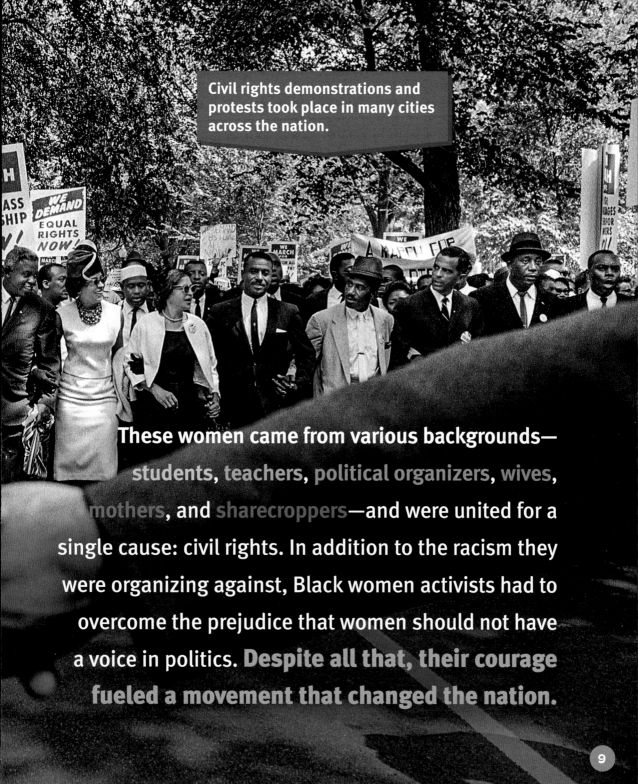

Civil rights demonstrations and protests took place in many cities across the nation.

These women came from various backgrounds—students, teachers, political organizers, wives, mothers, and sharecroppers—and were united for a single cause: civil rights. In addition to the racism they were organizing against, Black women activists had to overcome the prejudice that women should not have a voice in politics. Despite all that, their courage fueled a movement that changed the nation.

After paying their fares, Black passengers often had to exit the bus and reenter through the back door.

Segregation laws prevented Black and white people from using the same public spaces, such as bathrooms, water fountains, and movie theaters.

A Watershed Moment

In 1954, Montgomery, Alabama, was one of the most segregated cities in the U.S. Black children couldn't attend school with white children. The city buses were also segregated. The front seats were for white passengers only. Black riders sat in the back and were forced to give their seats to white passengers if the whites-only section filled up.

Rosa Parks

On December 1, 1955, Rosa Parks, a 42-year-old seamstress, boarded a city bus in Montgomery. When a white bus driver ordered her to give up her seat to a white man, she refused. Parks was fed up. African Americans paid the same fare as white people to ride the buses. Why shouldn't they sit where they pleased? Parks was arrested and taken to jail.

Rosa Parks was jailed twice—first for refusing to give up her seat and later as one of the bus boycott leaders.

Rosa Parks was a trained activist and a member of the NAACP. Though her actions had not been planned, her arrest lit a spark. The Women's Political Council (WPC), an activist organization in Montgomery created to combat racism, was led by Jo Ann Robinson. She had been preparing a campaign to **boycott** the city buses months before. Now that Parks, a soft-spoken churchgoer and well-respected member of the community, had been arrested, the WPC decided it was time to act.

About 40,000 African Americans participated in the boycott on December 5, 1955.

The majority of Montgomery's bus riders were Black women. Some worked as maids and cooks for wealthy white families. Many walked to work during the boycott.

Boycott

Robinson worked through the night, writing and printing a leaflet that urged Black riders to boycott the buses on Monday, December 5, four days after the arrest of Rosa Parks. The WPC circulated more than 50,000 copies of the leaflet throughout the Black community. Black people were the main passengers on the buses. If they refused to ride, the city would lose money. On December 5, city buses ran nearly empty, costing the city of Montgomery hundreds of dollars.

Committed for Change

That night, boycott leaders led a mass meeting at Holt Street Baptist Church. The one-day boycott had been a success, but the buses were still segregated. Should they continue the boycott? Many of the bus riders were Black women who worked as cooks, maids, and caregivers. They would have to walk long miles on tired feet every day if the boycott continued. Despite the hardship, the determined crowd voted to keep the boycott alive.

Some women and men carpooled to work during the Montgomery bus boycott.

An Early Victory

The Montgomery bus boycott lasted for 381 days, until the Supreme Court ruled that segregated buses were unconstitutional. The boycott was officially ended on December 20, 1956. The day after, Rosa Parks sat at the front of a desegregated bus for the first time. The success of the Montgomery bus boycott was a watershed moment for the growing civil rights movement. It inspired others to keep working for justice.

Rosa Parks (in dark coat) waits to board a bus after the boycott in Montgomery ended.

Police photos of some of the many women who were arrested for demonstrating for civil rights. Rosa Parks is seen in the bottom right photograph.

Even though the bus boycott was a success, there were repercussions. Many protesters lost their jobs. Churches and homes owned by Black leaders were bombed. Parks and Robinson received death threats. After the bus boycott, it was difficult for Parks to find work. But both leaders, along with all the other protesters, persevered in their fight for justice.

In the 1930s
the NAACP began a
campaign to use the
courts to desegregate
the nation's schools.

Enforce the Law!

Even before the bus boycott, Black people had been fighting for basic civil rights. One of those battles sought to overturn a Supreme Court ruling called *Plessy v. Ferguson*. In 1896, that case had ruled that "separate but equal" facilities for Black people and white people were legal. In practice, the facilities provided for Black Americans were never equal to those for white people. They were worse. This was especially true of schools.

Some Black youth joined the civil rights fight with their parents; others defied their parents by getting involved.

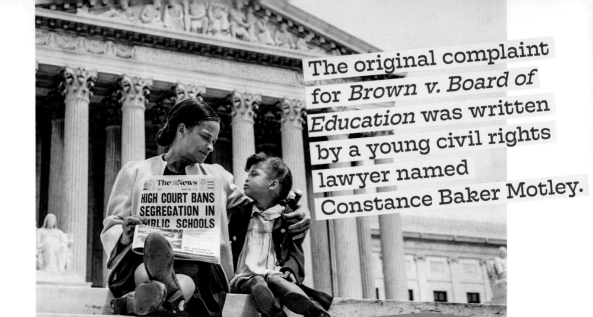

The original complaint for *Brown v. Board of Education* was written by a young civil rights lawyer named Constance Baker Motley.

A young mother sits with her daughter on the steps of the Supreme Court, holding a newspaper announcing the ban on segregation in public schools.

Brown v. Board of Education

On May 17, 1954, the NAACP won a major victory. In a decision called *Brown v. Board of Education of Topeka, Kansas,* the Supreme Court ruled that segregation in public schools was unconstitutional. Black and white students were now required to attend school together. But cities across the U.S. were slow to **integrate**. Some even refused.

First Steps

One of those cities was Little Rock, Arkansas. Daisy Bates, president of the Arkansas NAACP, was determined to see the state's schools integrated. In 1957, the Little Rock school district was forced to obey the new federal law. On September 4 that same year, Bates guided nine Black high school students— six girls and three boys—as they integrated Little Rock Central High School.

National guard troops escort and protect the Little Rock Nine as they prepare to enter Little Rock Central High School.

Due to a missed phone call, Elizabeth Eckford, one of the Little Rock Nine, arrived alone on the first day of school at Central High. The crowd shouted racial slurs at her.

The Little Rock Nine

Called the Little Rock Nine, the students endured racial slurs, emotional abuse, and physical danger from the white students and teachers daily. Bates's home became the central meeting place for the Little Rock Nine. She mentored them on how to remain strong and focused in the face of hate. Her home was repeatedly attacked, and she feared for her safety.

Some sit-in demonstrators completed college assignments while waiting to be served at lunch counters.

The Belles of Liberty

In the fall of 1959, young women from Bennett College in Greensboro, North Carolina, planned the first student **sit-in** at a local store called Woolworth's. African Americans shopped at Woolworth's, but they were refused service at the store's lunch counter. The women's group, known as the Belles of Liberty, decided to organize protesters to "sit in" at the counter until the laws barring Black people were changed. The first sit-in was staged on February 1, 1960.

Ella Baker's activism was inspired by the stories her grandmother had told of her life as an enslaved woman.

Ella Baker trained energetic college students, like Diane Nash, to be civil rights leaders.

Action!

Ella Baker was a fearless activist who worked for the NAACP throughout the segregated South beginning in the 1940s. When she first learned of the Montgomery bus boycott, she founded In Friendship, an organization that raised funds to support the protesters. Inspired by the boycott's success, Baker helped start the Southern Christian Leadership Conference (SCLC) to lead more civil rights protests.

Ella Baker

Baker used her skills to train young people to become leaders and activists. She often clashed with the male SCLC leaders, like Dr. Martin Luther King Jr. Many of them were not used to working with a woman on an equal level. Frustrated, she thought about resigning. But then the lunch counter sit-ins began, reenergizing Baker and her cause.

A woman is arrested and carried to a police wagon during a civil rights demonstration in New York in 1963.

Expanding the Movement

News of the sit-ins spread across the country. Diane Nash, a bold and brave college student, led 40 demonstrators in a sit-in at a Woolworth's lunch counter in Nashville, Tennessee, in February 1960. In retaliation, the home of a Black lawyer helping the protesters was bombed. Nash confronted the city's mayor, who agreed that it was wrong to segregate lunch counters. Later that year, Black people were finally served at Nashville lunch counters.

Diane Nash, right, was jailed in Mississippi for 10 days while she was pregnant with her first child.

The Birth of SNCC

By April, however, Ella Baker and other SCLC leaders feared the sit-ins and protests would fizzle out without better organization. They invited hundreds of student leaders to a weekend conference on the campus of Shaw University in North Carolina. The students were encouraged to start their own civil rights group, and on April 15, 1960, the Student Nonviolent Coordinating Committee (SNCC) was created.

Gloria Richardson, a civil rights activist, led protests in Maryland. Once, police gassed her and other marchers.

In 1960, in Atlanta, Georgia, African American women protested outside a department store that had a segregated lunch counter.

Diane Nash and other SNCC leaders organized nationwide sit-ins across the country. Building on the success of the lunch counter protests, Nash planned sit-ins in other segregated public spaces like libraries, swimming pools, and bus waiting areas. By September 1961, at least 70,000 Black and white demonstrators, women and men, had actively participated in the sit-ins.

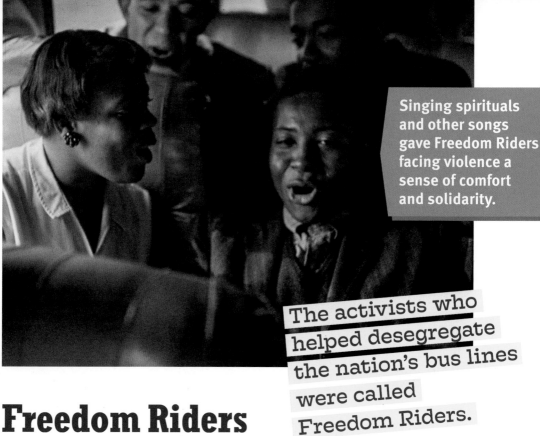

Singing spirituals and other songs gave Freedom Riders facing violence a sense of comfort and solidarity.

The activists who helped desegregate the nation's bus lines were called Freedom Riders.

Freedom Riders

In 1961, Nash planned another phase of protests called the Freedom Rides. Organized by the Congress of Racial Equality (CORE), Black and white activists boarded buses that traveled throughout the Southern states, challenging the segregated buses and waiting rooms along the nation's highways. Their goal was to make sure new laws overturning segregation were enforced.

The Freedom Riders faced extreme acts of violence. Many riders were jailed. Black activist and attorney Constance Motley traveled to the jails to get them out. President John F. Kennedy called in National Guard troops to protect the protesters as they traveled to Jackson, Mississippi.

In 1961, a bus carrying Freedom Riders was bombed outside of Anniston, Alabama.

The March on Washington

The March on Washington for Jobs and Freedom on August 28, 1963, was one of the most important moments of the civil rights movement. More than 250,000 women and men gathered in Washington, D.C., to pressure the government to pass civil rights legislation. Martin Luther King Jr. gave a speech proclaiming his dream for racial equality. Besides participating in the march, this is how women contributed to this key historical moment.

Volunteering

Black women's groups around the country arranged for hundreds of women volunteers to travel to Washington to help with food preparation, clean-up, and support for the thousands of protesters who would march against racism.

Protesters gather on the National Mall in Washington, D.C., to support civil rights legislation.

SEEK THE
EEDO

Organization

Dorothy Height (pictured), president of the National Council of Negro Women, and Anna Arnold Hedgeman of the National Council of Churches were the only two women among the male leaders who organized the march. They rallied the male members of the organizing committee to allow Black women activists to sit on the stage and have an opportunity to speak at the march.

Public Speaking

The day of the march, a few women were sitting on the stage but only one woman was allowed to give a speech during the official program. She was Daisy Bates (pictured), the mentor to the Little Rock Nine and president of the Arkansas chapter of the NAACP. She promised that women would continue to protest until every school in the country was integrated and Black people had equal access to the vote.

Despite their hard work, Black women were sidelined on the day of the march. The female leaders had to march separately from the male leaders. Black leaders attended a White House meeting with President Kennedy, but no women were invited.

The motto of the National Association of Colored Women's Clubs, formed in 1896, was "Lifting as We Climb."

The daughter of former enslaved people, Mary McLeod Bethune (center) was an important civil and women's rights activist.

Uniting for the Vote

Starting in the early 1800s, American women banded together to fight for their right to vote. This was called the women's suffrage movement. However, racism made it difficult for Black women to join the suffrage movement. So Black women created their own organizations, known collectively as the Women's Club Movement, to advocate for themselves and their communities.

In 1869, the Fifteenth Amendment to the Constitution gave African American men the right to vote. But it was not until 1920 that the Nineteenth Amendment granted women the same right. Even after all Americans had the legal right to vote, segregationists created barriers to prevent African Americans from voting. States passed poll taxes and literacy laws that required people to pay a tax or know how to read if they wanted to vote.

Barriers to Voting

African Americans were threatened with violence when they tried to register to vote. They were forced to return to registration offices over and over again to prove they had a legal right to vote. Mary McLeod Bethune, an educator and activist, formed the National Council of Negro Women in 1935 to pursue equal access to voting for African Americans. She protested poll taxes and taught school classes to help Black voters pass literacy tests.

A woman adding her vote to the ballot box in Baltimore, Maryland, in 1964.

A New Party

In 1962, Fannie Lou Hamer, a civil rights worker, joined SNCC leaders and became one of many women who volunteered in the campaign to register Black voters. Ordinary citizens who worked as hairdressers, teachers, and housewives faced difficult and dangerous conditions in this campaign. Women were shot at, beaten, and arrested when attempting to register.

Women and men who helped register Black voters in the 1960s faced extreme violence. Some even lost their lives.

On national television, Fanny Lou Hamer detailed the awful beating she suffered in jail for her civil rights work.

Too Young to Vote But Not to March

On May 2, 1963, more than 3,000 Black children left their schools in Birmingham, Alabama, to join a protest march known as the Children's Crusade. Among them was nine-year-old Audrey Faye Hendricks, the youngest known marcher. Their goal was to pressure the city into lifting its segregation laws. Audrey was arrested and jailed along with many other young people. Americans watched TV news footage of children sprayed with fire hoses, attacked by police dogs, and jailed. On May 10, the city was persuaded to desegregate its businesses and release the young protesters from jail.

Black youth marched, went to jail, and some even lost their lives in the struggle for equal rights.

Legacy of the Movement

In 1964, the Civil Rights Act was passed, barring segregation in public places and **discrimination** based on race. One year later, the Voting Rights Act, which outlawed discriminatory voting practices, was passed. Black women activists also helped fuel future social justice movements for marginalized peoples throughout our nation and the world.

Timeline: Women and the Civil Rights Movement

December 1
Rosa Parks's arrest inspires the Montgomery bus boycott.

Activist Ella Baker acts as a mentor to student leaders of SNCC, who begin planning protests around the country.

1954 — **1955** — **1957** — **1960**

Attorney Constance Motley writes the original complaint that leads to *Brown v. Board of Education of Topeka, Kansas.*

September 23
The Little Rock Nine become the first African American students to integrate Little Rock Central High School. Six of the nine are young women.

Unfortunately, racial discrimination still exists in our nation. The Black Lives Matter movement, founded in 2012 by three African American women, organizes protests against the shootings of unarmed Black citizens by police officers. Many believe that the United States still has much work to do before all Americans share true equality. 🇺🇸

The Voting Rights Act is signed. Women like Fannie Lou Hamer lead voting drives throughout the South.

1963

1964

1965

August 28
Civil rights activists hold the March on Washington for Jobs and Freedom. Most women's contributions are unacknowledged.

July 2
President Lyndon B. Johnson signs the Civil Rights Act into law. The original bill did not include barring discrimination on the basis of sex.

More Women and Girls Who Shaped the Civil Rights Movement

Mary Ann Shadd Cary (1823–1893)

A political activist, abolitionist, and suffragist, she advocated for freedom and education for Black people and women. Her work inspired civil rights activists of the 1940s and 1950s.

Ida B. Wells (1862–1931)

A journalist, suffragist, and activist, she was a founding member of the NAACP. Her work to expose lynchings in the South brought national attention to the treatment and lack of rights of Black people.

Mary Church Terrell (1863–1954)

The daughter of former slaves, she was one of the first African American women to earn a college degree and became known as a national activist for civil rights and suffrage.

Barbara Rose Johns (1935–1991)

In 1951, 15-year-old Barbara Johns, who attended school in a segregated tar paper shack, led her fellow students in a boycott to draw attention to the unfair school conditions. Their protest became part of the *Brown v. Board of Education* lawsuit that led to the desegregation of schools in 1954.

Coretta Scott King (1927–2006)

The wife of Dr. Martin Luther King Jr. and a civil rights activist, she founded the King Center and was instrumental in making her husband's birthday a federal holiday.

Charlayne Hunter-Gault (born 1942)

She faced down racist taunts and riots as the first Black woman to enter the University of Georgia in 1961.

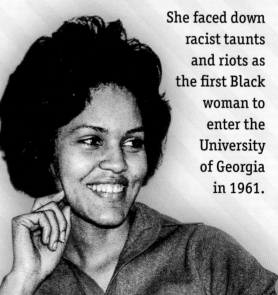

True Statistics

The number of African Americans who boycotted the Montgomery buses on the first day of the boycott: **about 40,000**

The number of Black and white demonstrators who actively participated in sit-ins: **at least 70,000**

The number of children arrested during the Children's Crusade of 1963: **500+**

The number of protesters who joined the March on Washington for Jobs and Freedom: **250,000+**

The number of senators who voted to pass the Civil Rights Act: **77 out of 100**

The number of African American citizens in the United States in 1960 according to the U.S. Census: **18,800,000 or 10.5 percent of the population**

Did you find the truth?

T The Montgomery bus boycott was organized by a woman.

F Daisy Bates was one of three female speakers at the March on Washington for Jobs and Freedom in 1963.

Resources

Further Reading

Allen, Zita. *Black Women Leaders of the Civil Rights Movement.* New York: Grolier Publishing, 1996.

Bell, Janet Dewart. *Lighting the Fires of Freedom: African American Women in the Civil Rights Movement.* New York: The New Press, 2018.

Levinson, Cynthia. *The Youngest Marcher: The Story of Audrey Faye Hendricks, a Young Civil Rights Activist.* New York: Atheneum Books, 2017.

Weatherford, Carole Boston. *Voice of Freedom: Fannie Lou Hamer, Spirit of the Civil Rights Movement.* Somerville, MA: Candlewick Press, 2015.

Other Books in the Series

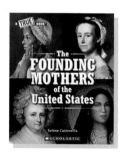
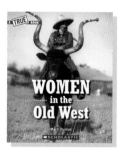
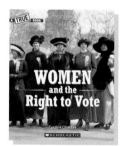
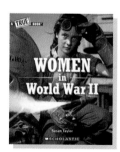

Glossary

activists (AK-tuh-vists) people who support a cause and take action to achieve reform

boycott (BOI-kaht) to refuse to do business as a punishment or protest

civil disobedience (SIV-uhl dis-oh-BEE-dee-uhns) the act of disobeying a law on the grounds of moral or political principle

civil rights (SIV-uhl rites) the individual rights to freedom and equal treatment under the law granted to all members of a democratic society

discrimination (dis-krim-i-NAY-shuhn) prejudice or unfair behavior to others based on differences in such things as age, race, or gender

integrate (IN-ti-grayt) to open facilities or an organization to people of all races and ethnic groups

nonviolent protest (non-VY-lent PRO-test) a peaceful way to express disapproval of a law of policy

segregation (seg-re-GAY-shuhn) the act or practice of keeping people or groups apart based on differences in such things as age, race, or gender

sit-in (SIT-in) the occupation of a place by an individual or group as a form of protest

Index

Page numbers in **bold** indicate illustrations.

About the Author

Kesha Grant's favorite pastimes as a child were reading books and playing school with her neighborhood friends, so it seems only fitting that she became a writer and a teacher. When she was in the sixth grade, Kesha wrote her first book and entered it into a school-wide contest. Though she didn't win, Kesha got her first taste of authorship and has been in love with writing ever since. She recently received her MFA in Writing for Children and Young Adults from Hamline University. She writes true accounts of unsung heroes whose stories never made it into history books she read as a child. When not writing, she enjoys cooking and spending time with her family. She resides in Atlanta, Georgia.